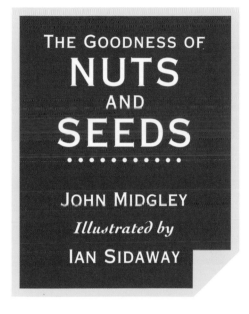

THE GOODNESS OF
NUTS
AND
SEEDS

JOHN MIDGLEY

Illustrated by

IAN SIDAWAY

RANDOM HOUSE
NEW YORK

ACKNOWLEDGEMENTS
The author thanks Sue Midgley and Jo Swinnerton
for kindly checking the text.

FURTHER READING
Jill Norman's excellent *Complete Book of Spices*, and *Nuts*
(both published by Dorling Kindersley).
For those interested in reading more about food and health
The Food Pharmacy, by Jean Carper (Simon and Schuster)
and *Superfoods*, by Michael Van Straten and
Barbara Griggs (Dorling Kindersley) are recommended.
Reay Tannahill's *Food in History* (Penguin) is recommended
to all with an interest in the history of food.
A New Book of Middle Eastern Food,
by Claudia Roden (published by Viking)
is excellent on the nutty foods of that region.

Published in the United States by Random House, Inc., New York.

This work was published in Great Britain by
Pavilion Books Limited, London.

ISBN 0-679-42681-7

Library of Congress Cataloging-in-Publication Data is available.

Manufactured in Hong Kong

2 4 6 8 9 7 5 3

First U.S. Edition

CONTENTS

· · · · · · · · · · ·

PART
ONE

. . . .

NUTS AND SEEDS

· · · · · · · · · ·

Nuts and seeds were gathered in the wild by our earliest ancestors. The trees and plants on which they fruit grow wild in many different climates, and are cultivated in various parts of the world, for oil extraction (many nuts and some seeds have an extremely high fat content and yield very good oil), and for all manner of culinary uses.

The botanical definition of a nut is a fruit with a dry, hard shell that has to be cracked open to release a solitary edible kernel. Cashews, chestnuts and hazelnuts fall within this category. Ordinarily, however, the term is used less precisely and covers other edible fruits with a hard shell, including coconuts, as well as some plant seeds such as pine nuts, Brazil nuts, and pistachio nuts, and a legume (the peanut). Some more obvious plant seeds such as sunflower and pumpkin are nutty in character (and, like some nuts, are grown for oil) while others are familiar spices.

Most of the world's cuisines make some use of the nuts and seeds available to them, which is determined by differing climatic and historical factors. For example, almonds and pine nuts appear in diverse forms throughout southern Europe; pistachios are favoured in the Middle East; pecans in North America; walnuts, hazelnuts and chestnuts are popular in temperate and warm parts of Europe; and coconuts, candlenuts, peanuts, cashews and macadamia nuts are widely used in tropical countries. Small dried plant seeds are equally versatile. Nuts and seeds are essential ingredients in many cakes, biscuits, pastries, confectionery, desserts and ice creams, pilaffs and pilaus, stews, braises, tagines, curries, pies, sauces, pestos, breads, flours and meals, stuffings and purées, drinks, and pickles and preserves, not forgetting their value as simple snack or dessert foods.

The nutritional value of most nuts and seeds is primarily as rich sources of (largely mono- and polyunsaturated) fats, protein, vitamins, and minerals. One, the chestnut, is starchy, and has saved thousands of European peasant farmers from starvation when wheat has been scarce. Many seeds are valued also in traditional medicines, especially in India and China, where they are believed to have heating and cooling properties, as well as specific therapeutic uses to treat individual ailments, such as migraine, asthma and digestive disorders.

Nuts

Almonds

The almond tree (*Prunus amygdalus* var. *dulcis*) is related to the peach and plum, and is probably native to the eastern Mediterranean. Today, almond trees are widely cultivated in all the Mediterranean countries, as well as further afield where the climate is suitably Mediterranean such as California, South Africa, parts of Australia, Chile and Argentina. They are important nuts commercially, and, with their high fat content are the source of a delicate oil. Almonds are used in a wide variety of cakes and biscuits, desserts and confectionery, but also to thicken savoury foods such as soups, sauces and stews; they are chopped to garnish fish and poultry, and roasted and salted, to be eaten as a snack. Almonds may be bought sugared or salted, blanched and left whole, or halved, slivered, flaked, or ground. Marzipan is made with water, sugar and crushed almonds. Bitter almonds (*Prunus amygdalus* var. *amara*) contain prussic acid and are toxic when raw; they are distilled to produce real almond essence.

Brazil nuts

These large nuts with their characteristic three-sided shells are the seeds of huge fruits produced by *Bertholletia excelsa*, a tall tree that is native to the Amazonian rain forests, a large part of which belongs to Brazil, as the name reflects. Each fruit contains up to two dozen seeds. With their very high fat content, Brazil nuts turn rancid quite quickly. They are seldom used in savoury dishes, but are eaten as dessert nuts, or grated, chopped or ground, and added to cakes and biscuits. Their main commercial value is to the confectionery industry.

Candlenuts

Not to be confused with macadamia nuts, these small, round tropical nuts (*Aleurites moluccana*) are mildly toxic when raw, and used primarily to thicken Indonesian curries and stews, once they have been ground or crushed. High in fat, they are prone to turning rancid. They are unlikely to be found outside specialist Oriental stores, where they can be bought already shelled and where they are sometimes labelled under their Indonesian name, *kemiri*.

Cashews

Cashews grow on *Anacardium occidentale*, a tree native to South America that is related to the mango and the pistachio. They are among the most widely cultivated nuts, and are grown throughout the tropics, including South America, parts of Africa, India, and the Far East, where they are especially popular. High in fat, they can be ground to an oily paste, roasted and salted to be eaten as a snack, or combined with poultry or vegetable stir-fries. Cashews are rarely available unshelled, but can be bought raw, or roasted. Unsalted cashews are best in cooking.

Chestnuts

Native to southern Europe, the sweet chestnut (*Castanea sativa*) has been a vital source of starch in some impoverished parts of Europe; in France, it is still called 'the bread tree' (*l'arbre à pain*), after the floury nuts which are very low in fat. Varieties of sweet chestnut grow in many different parts of the world, also producing edible nuts, although they should not be confused with the horse chestnut (*Aesculus hippocastanum*) whose nuts are inedible. In parts of northern Italy, and in Corsica, coarsely ground chestnut meal is also cooked in boiling water as polenta. As well as being a popular ingredient in stuffings and an appetizing vegetable in their own right, chestnuts are favoured in dessert-making and confectionery-making; marrons glacés are a luxury sweet consisting of shelled chestnuts preserved in syrup. Peeling chestnuts is made easier this way: score a cross on the flat sides of the shells, then fry them briefly before roasting them for a short time. This will loosen the shells and skins. Peeled chestnuts are available dried and need to be rehydrated by several hours' soaking in water; alternatively, peeled whole French chestnuts may be bought in vacuum-sealed cans. Chestnut flour can be bought in some Italian delicatessens.

Coconuts

The fruits of the coconut palm (*Cocos nucuifera*) are among the most valued of nuts, by virtue of their immense versatility, culinary and otherwise, their year-round availability, and their widespread distribution throughout the tropics. Immature, green coconuts are rarely seen outside their native lands. Within is a refreshing drink and a delicious snack; the tops are sliced off with a machete, and a segment of the shell serves as a scoop for the soft, gelatinous, low-fat flesh, once the cool, clear juice has been drunk. Mature coconuts have developed hard brown shells covered in a tough fibre that is used to make rope and matting. Their hard, fatty white flesh, known as copra when it is dried specifically for oil extraction, is also dried and sold as desiccated coconut, which, when soaked, produces coconut milk. Coconut oil, though excellent for frying, is high in saturated fats. Canned coconut 'milk', made and exported primarily by Thailand, the Philippines and Indonesia, is a concentrated cream made with coconut flesh that is widely used in southeast Asian and south Indian curries and sauces. Dry, compressed blocks of coconut cream are equally suitable, and can be diluted with boiling water.

Hazelnuts

Hazel (*Corylus avellana*) is native to temperate parts of Europe, while the Turkish hazel (*Corylus colurna*), and the filbert (*Corylus maxima*) are native to the eastern Mediterranean. Cobs are nuts that are sold very fresh, while still in their green husks, and are especially delicious. Trees of the *Corylus* genus are rather small and bushy, the tallest being the Turkish hazel which can reach a height of 25 metres/82 feet. In England, wild hazel is commonly found in hedgerows, and the county of Kent is famous for its cultivated filberts, misleadingly called 'cob nuts'. Hazel wood is prized for carving, and makes sturdy sticks. Hazelnuts, being high in fat, also yield an expensive salad oil of excellent quality and flavour. The nuts are popular, especially in Catalonia where they are used in picadas (aromatic pastes of nuts, garlic and fresh herbs). They are also indispensable in many kinds of confectionery, including chocolate, some kinds of nougat, and as pastry fillings.

Macadamia nuts

These nuts are native to the tropical rainforest of the north-eastern Australian state of Queensland, where they grow on a tree called *Macadamia ternifolia*. For this reason, they are also commonly known as Queensland nuts. Invariably sold shelled and vacuum-packed because of their high oil content, which rapidly turns them rancid, they are usually imported from Hawaii, now the leading grower. They are delicious lightly salted and eaten as a snack, but may also be ground to thicken sauces, especially south-east Asian ones.

Peanuts

Also known as the groundnut, or monkey nut, the peanut (*Arachis hypogaea*) is truly a legume, like the pea after which it is named. The 'shell' is in fact the dried bean pod, and the 'nut', the dried seed of the plant. Native to South America, peanuts, undoubtedly the most commercially important of all the nuts mentioned here, are now cultivated in many different hot regions including the southern states of North America, West Africa, India, China, Malaysia, and Indonesia. Moderately high in fat, they are equally valued for their cooking oil, which is indispensable in frying, and in Chinese cooking. Peanuts are perhaps the most universally popular snack nut, and are sold shelled and left raw; roasted, salted, and shelled; and unshelled. Peanuts are extremely versatile in cooking, and appear in many Oriental dishes, such as Chinese *kung pao* chicken, Indonesian *bumbu*, a sauce that invariably accompanies satay, and *gado gado*, a rich peanut dress-

11

ing for boiled eggs and lightly cooked vegetables, as well as chilli-hot West African stews and soups. In the United States peanuts are also widely cultivated for the peanut butter industry.

Pecans

A variety of hickory, the pecan (*Carya illinoensis*) is native to North America where it is cultivated today. With their ridged grooves, the shelled nuts resemble small, streamlined walnut meats, while the shells themselves are smooth, reddish ovals. Sold shelled and unshelled, they have a very high fat content and easily go rancid. They are used in ice cream, baking (and make a delicious bread) and as a topping for cakes, but are best celebrated in the all-American classic, pecan pie. They are also a good snack nut.

Pine Nuts

Pine nuts are the seeds of *Pinus pinea*, the Mediterranean stone pine. These delicious, pale little nuts, sometimes also known as pine kernels (meats) or pine seeds, are essential ingredients in Spanish, Italian, Greek, Turkish and Middle Eastern cookery.

The seeds or kernels shelter between the 'leaves' of the pine cones, so harvesting them is laborious and expensive. High in fat, they tend to turn rancid unless used quickly, but their expense is a deterrent to overstocking. Because of their high fat content, they are also harvested for oil extraction, but the high costs involved are reflected in the price of the product which, though excellent and highly aromatic, is quite rare. In cookery, pine nuts excel in fragrant Ligurian pesto, in Catalan picadas, and are frequently added to rice pilaffs. They are also delicious added to leafy salads, to cooked spinach, and other vegetables. Mixed with cooked rice and spiced, minced meat, they are used to stuff garden vegetables and vine leaves, and feature in many Mediterranean cakes, biscuits and pastries.

Pistachios

Native to Persia and neighbouring parts of the Middle East, *Pistacia vera* produces pale green nuts with purplish skins that are clearly visible when their hard shells split open on drying. They are the finest snack nuts, and are especially popular in Balkan and Middle Eastern countries where they are sold by street vendors and from kiosks. They are a popular thickening agent, and the source of a green food colouring. Widely used in stuffings and desserts, they are perhaps most famous in Italian pistachio ice cream. Although they have a high fat content pistachio oil is only rarely encountered.

Walnuts

Walnuts have been cultivated since antiquity, not only for their nuts but also for their exquisitely whorled timber, which is used in veneering and cabinet-making. The principal species are *Juglans regia* (English or California walnut), *Juglans nigra* (black or American walnut), and *Juglans cinera* (butternut). They are grown intensively in south-west France, northern Italy, and California, and, being high in fat, are also an important salad oil crop. Among the most important and popular of nuts, walnuts can be picked green for pickling, or allowed to mature and harvested in autumn (fall). 'Wet' walnuts are delicious, tender, young walnuts that have not been allowed to dry out; highly perishable, they are available only in a short season. Dried, unshelled walnuts keep well and are more likely to be available. Walnut kernels (meats) are also sold shelled, chopped and ground. Walnut oil is the most highly prized of all salad oils, and the best comes from France. Expensive, but concentrated in flavour, it should be used sparingly, although it perishes quickly. For that reason it is often sold in relatively small containers. Walnuts are supremely versatile, and their culinary uses are legion, from bread, cakes, biscuits, chocolate and confectionery, to pie fillings, sauces, pestos and picadas. They are excellent in salads (dressed with walnut oil), in stuffing and on their own; combined simply with slivers of parmesan and torn fresh basil leaves, they are an exquisite canapé.

Seeds

Alfalfa

A major animal feed crop, and an ancient cultivated vegetable, the sprouted seeds of *Medicago sativa* are exceptionally nutritious, being rich in protein, vitamins, minerals and fibre, and are used chiefly in salads.

Aniseed

Pimpinella anisum is native to the Mediterranean where it grows profusely, filling the warm summer air with its perfume of liquorice. The seeds, which are similar to fennel seeds, are used primarily to extract oil for various liqueurs such as Spanish *anis*, and French *pastis*. In India, the seeds are chewed to refresh the palate.

Caraway

The crescent-shaped seeds of *Carum carvi* are especially identified with the cuisines of central and northern European countries, where they are used to flavour rye breads, cakes, cheeses and some savoury soups and stews.

Cardamom

The dried pods of *Elettaria cardamomum* harbour seeds that are used to flavour many Indian rice dishes and curries, and are ground with other spices to make *garam masala*. The white (bleached), green, or black pods are also popular in North Africa and the Middle East where they flavour coffee.

Celery

Apium graveolens is best known as a stalk and root vegetable, but its tiny dried seeds are used commercially to flavour pickles, preserves, ketchups and relishes, and domestically, to flavour soups and stews, particularly in northern Europe.

Coriander (cilantro)

The seeds of *Coriandrum sativum* are among the most popular and widely used of spices. They are essential in many Arab and Indian spice mixtures, and are used whole, and ground. Europeans use whole coriander seeds mainly in pickling, and the French include them in vegetables cooked *à la greeque*.

Cumin

Cumin seeds come from *Cuminum cyminum*, a plant native to Egypt. They are a popular spice, both whole and ground, and, like coriander seeds (with which they are often combined) are an essential Indian spice. They are also used in Mexican cooking, and throughout North Africa and the Middle East.

Dill

Dill seeds are the dried fruits of one of northern Europe's most popular fresh herbs, *Anethum graveolens*. Their popularity extends from India to Scandinavia and the seeds are used in much the same way as caraway seeds.

Fennel

The seeds of *Foeniculum vulgare* are strongly aromatic. They are deftly used in Indian spicing, as well as in their native Mediterranean lands, and are a useful pickling spice.

Fenugreek

Native to Asia minor, *Trigonella foenum-graecum* produces blunt little pale orange seeds that are mostly associated with various Indian and Sri Lankan spice mixtures. They are highly nutritious when sprouted.

Mustard

Black, brown and white mustard seeds are the products of varieties of *brassica*, and are ground to make mustards. A pickling spice, the seeds also feature in Indian dishes. Frying in hot oil makes them pop, and releases their pungent and nutty flavour. Mustard oil is popular in India where it is often used in place of ghee (clarified butter).

Poppy

The seeds of *Papaver somniferum* (the opium poppy) are used mainly in baking, although they are also a source of salad oil. The seeds are tiny, round pellets and can be cream, brown, or slate grey. They are suitable for sprouting, when they become particularly nutritious. Although opium oozes from the unripe pods when cut, it is absent from the mature seeds.

Pumpkin

Pumpkins (*Cucurbita maxima*) are a native American plant whose seeds are the source of a thick, very dark brown oil, but are also roasted and eaten as a snack. Pumpkin seeds may also be sprouted.

Rape

Brassica napus is widely cultivated for oil extraction, especially in more northerly temperate countries that are inhospitable to other oil-yielding plants. Rapeseed oil is light and bland and well suited to most culinary uses.

Sesame

The seeds of the sesame plant (*Sesamum indicum*) have been crushed for oil for thousands of years, and are also widely used in cooking. Two kinds of oil are available: light, cold-pressed oil, and thick, dark Oriental sesame oil; the latter is extracted from toasted seeds, and is widely used in small quantities to season Chinese, Japanese and Korean dishes. The beige, white or black seeds, which are sometimes sprouted, are chiefly used to decorate or coat breads and other foods. They are also crushed to make Middle Eastern tahina paste, and *halvah*. In the Far East they are lightly toasted and added to dishes to impart a nutty flavour and crunchy texture. They are also widely used in Indian cooking.

Sunflower

Native to South America, the sunflower (*Helianthus annuus*) is an important crop in many parts of Europe, chiefly for the light cooking oil that is extracted from its seeds. High in polyunsaturated and monounsaturated fats, bland sunflower oil is widely used in frying and as a salad oil. In many Mediterranean countries, roasted and salted sunflower seeds in their shells are a popular children's snack. Sunflower seeds may also be sprouted and added to salads, being highly nutritious and pleasantly nutty.

The Goodness of Nuts and Seeds

Nuts and seeds are highly nutritious. Rich in protein, and an excellent source of energy in the form of fat, their mainly polyunsaturated and monounsaturated fatty acids (present in solid nuts and seeds and their oils) are linked with cardiovascular disease prevention. They also provide essential vitamins and minerals. Sprouted seeds are exceptionally nutritious and provide a rich package of essential nutrients, including protein, vitamins and minerals, and are high in fibre.

Protein is vital to health and is usually obtained from meat, fish and dairy products. However, for many, nuts are an essential source of protein that can be paired with vegetable protein, carbohydrates and foods rich in vitamin C that facilitate their absorption. Many West Africans rely on peanuts for protein when meat, fish or fowl are unavailable, and the world's vegetarian communities get their protein from certain nuts and seeds, as well as fresh and dried legumes, and dairy products. Of the seeds, sesame, sunflower and pumpkin seeds are especially protein-rich.

Fats can be mainly saturated (as animal fats and their derivatives are), polyunsaturated (like some vegetable oils), or monounsaturated (like olive oil), or they can be a combination. Many doctors believe that diets that are high in saturated fats promote high blood cholesterol levels and contribute to cardiovascular disease, which remains one of the gravest threats to health in some parts of the western world. Countries that eschew saturated fats in favour of unsaturated ones have very low incidences of the disease. (Anomalies such as France may be explained by the protective effect of phenols in red wine, and by the presence of fish oils in the diet.) It is believed that the 'low density lipoprotein' (LDL) kind of blood cholesterol promotes fatty deposits in the blood vessels called *plaque* which can attract potentially fatal blood clots *(thromboses)*, cause the inner lining of the vessels to roughen, harden and narrow *(atherosclerosis)*, and raise blood pressure, thereby increasing the risk of heart attacks and strokes. Mono- and polyunsaturated vegetable fats reduce general blood cholesterol levels. However, another, beneficial kind of blood cholesterol known as 'high density lipoprotein' (HDL) helps to prevent plaque, dissolve thromboses, reduce atherosclerosis, and lower blood pressure. This kind is promoted by certain nuts and seeds, and their derivative oils that are high in monounsaturated fats, such as almonds, peanuts, hazelnuts, mustard seeds, pistachios, rapeseed, and sesame seeds. (Walnuts, sunflower seeds and pumpkin seeds and their oils are higher in polyunsaturates, but coconuts and coconut oil are very high in saturated fats.)

Numerous studies bear this out, including one conducted by the American Medical Association, which concluded in July 1992 that, of the subjects studied, those eating nuts more than five times a week ran a relatively low risk of heart disease, compared with infrequent consumers and abstainers. Nuts were shown to have a 'strong and consistent protective effect against coronary heart disease', according to the authors of the report.

The vitamin and mineral content of nuts and seeds varies considerably, but several (walnuts, almonds, peanuts, sesame and sunflower seeds) contain iron and zinc; almonds and walnuts also contain potassium; magnesium is found in almonds and Brazil nuts; B, B1 and B complex vitamins are present in almonds, Brazil nuts, pumpkin and sunflower seeds; and sesame seeds are rich in vitamin E, an anticarcinogenic antioxidant.

· · · · · · · · · ·

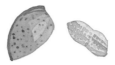

Phrase and etymology

*O God! I could be bounded in a nut-shell,
and count myself a king of infinite space,
were it not that I have bad dreams*
HAMLET

Quoting Cicero, Pliny claims that the *Iliad* was copied in a script so tiny as to be contained within the shell of a walnut, an experiment successfully conducted by Huet, Bishop of Avranches in the seventeenth century.

The phrase 'an old chestnut' (a stale joke) dates to a nineteenth century play entitled *The Broken Sword* by William Diamond. In the play one character forever tells different variations of the same joke, one of which concerns a cork tree. On hearing it, another character corrects him: 'A chestnut. I have heard you tell the joke twenty-seven times, and I am sure it was a chestnut.'

Our word almond and French *amande* derive from a medieval Latin word *amandula*. Also from Latin come chestnut (*chestaine* in Middle English, *chastaine* in Old French): *castanea* was 'the nut of Castaneae.' Pistachio (*pistace* in Middle English and Old French) derives from the Latin word *pistacium*, and ultimately from the Persian *pistah*. Our words for two American nuts are very close to their native Indian words: cashew and Portuguese *caju* from the Tupí *acaju*; and pecan from the Algonquian *paccan*. Finally, Old Norse is the source of the several English words. Nut derives from *hnot*; walnut is a compound of *wahlnot* ('foreign nut'); and hazel comes from Old Norse *hasl*.

A brief history of nuts and seeds

When nomadic hunter-gatherers first settled in small farming communities, and started to grow and cook food routinely (rather than opportunistically), a need was born for oils and fats. There is firm evidence that sesame oil was used in cooking, and coconuts were grown as fruits, at the height of the Indus Valley civilizations at Harappa and Mohenjo-Daro around 2300BC. However, it is very likely that sesame was cultivated much earlier in its native Africa, and in Mesopotamia and Persia at about the same time, or a little later. Spices too have been traded in the Mediterranean since the dawn of civilization, and according to an Egyptian papyrus dating to 1550BC, anise, caraway, cardamom, fenugreek, mustard and sesame seeds were all in circulation.

The Greeks extracted oil from walnuts and poppies before they acquired the olive, and valued various plant seeds medicinally, including coriander and cardamom (the latter in perfumery). The Romans grew almonds, pine nuts, walnuts and chestnuts, and imported pistachios. They used various plant seeds as spices and medicines, such as anise, caraway, cardamom, celery, coriander, cumin, fennel, mustard, and poppy (which was popular mixed with honey). They also grew fenugreek for animal fodder, calling it *foenum graecum*, 'the Greeks' hay.'

Aromatic seeds such as cardamom, coriander, cumin, fennel, mustard and sesame have been grown for many centuries in India where the tradition of cooking with spices is ancient. In China, sesame has been in continuous cultivation for some 2000 years, arriving from India in the Han period, together with walnuts, caraway and coriander, and alfalfa to feed the emperor Han Wu-ti's 'heavenly horses'.

The Persians' and Arabs' love of nuts and spices was, and remains, passionate. The Arabs were responsible for their introduction to regions that are famous today for their nutty sweets, such as Sicily and Spain. On conquering Persia they acquired almonds, which they introduced in turn into Spain. By AD900 the Arabs had become particularly inventive in their culinary use of nuts; sweet, nutty desserts such as nougat, nut sauces and pastes, and savoury dishes combining chopped or ground nuts with meat or poultry are Arab or Persian in origin. Almonds, pine nuts, walnuts and pistachios, and aromatic seeds such as cumin and coriander typify Middle Eastern cooking. In her influential book on the subject, *A New Book of Middle Eastern Food* (Viking) Claudia Roden identifies close similarities between many traditional European dishes – even some that are quintessentially English – and their Arab originals, explaining that returning Crusader knights hankered for the sophisticated foods of the east. (She singles out marzipan topping, mince pies, and Christmas pudding as examples!)

Much later, in the sixteenth century, the Moslem Mughals' passion for nuts left a permanent stamp upon the cuisine of northern India: their legacy includes rice pilaus containing nuts and seeds, almond sweetmeats, almond milk, sugary coconut confections, poultry stuffed with rice, almonds (or pistachios) and raisins, and *halvah*.

European food in the late Middle Ages was heavily spiced, and remained influenced by its Roman legacy. Spices were the preserve of the very rich, but even the poor could afford mustard, which can be cultivated in a cold climate, as can caraway, whose seeds were added to vegetables (a Roman habit first mentioned by Apicius). Coriander seeds were, and still are, used in pickling. The monasteries' herb and physic gardens grew many such herbs, including anise, whose seeds were important in medieval medicine.

The Aztecs of Mexico had grown sunflowers and pumpkins long before the Spaniards arrived, though it is uncertain if they knew how to extract oil from these seeds, or indeed from corn, another New World crop. The Incas of Peru also grew peanuts, which were a valuable source of protein in their largely meatless diet. The Spaniards and the Portuguese introduced peanuts to the Indies and by the beginning of the seventeenth century peanuts had reached China where they rapidly became an important crop. (Conversely, settlers brought coconuts from the east to the West Indies and to tropical America.) The Portuguese found cashews in South America, and introduced them to West Africa and to Goa, on India's west coast. Like peanuts, they quickly spread eastwards and soon became an important ingredient in Chinese cookery.

Pecans, a form of hickory, were known by North American Indians, and together with peanuts are now a significant cash crop in the warmer southern states. Chestnuts and walnuts were introduced into North America by European settlers, and are grown today in California, which is the leading producer of a blond variety of walnut called the butternut.

Many of the following recipes are from different countries where nuts and seeds are traditionally esteemed.

PART
TWO
· · · · · · · · · ·

Almond and Gorgonzola Canapés

These quick and easy canapés may also be served with a selection of hors d'oeuvres. In the Périgord region of France similar recipes call for walnuts and Roquefort cheese, and some Spanish tapas combine blue *cabrales* cheese with pine nuts. This makes about 20 canapés.

175g/6oz gorgonzola cheese, at room temperature
2 tsp brandy
50g/2oz whole, blanched almonds
2 sticks (ribs) of celery, washed and trimmed
leaves from a chicory (Belgian endive), washed and patted dry

Mash the gorgonzola with the brandy, which will quickly soften it. Lightly toast the almonds in a hot, dry pan, until golden. Chop them roughly, and mash them into the gorgonzola paste. Cut the celery into 6cm/2$\frac{1}{2}$ inch sections. Spread the mixture on to the concave sides of the celery and chicory, and serve. (May be prepared in advance.)

WALNUT, BASIL AND PARMESAN SNACKS

Serve these utterly delicious bite-size morsels with drinks; they accompany chilled champagne or sparkling wine perfectly. Only use good quality parmesan, and very fresh, 'wet' walnuts; stale or rancid nuts from a packet will ruin the flavour. The quantity makes twenty-four snacks.

12 walnuts
12 leaves of fresh basil, roughly torn
110g/4oz piece of parmesan

Stand the walnuts upright on a hard surface and tap the pointed ends with a hammer or mallet, to smash the shells. Separate the shells from the kernels (meats), but try to preserve intact halves. Slice the parmesan into little cubes or slivers roughly the same size as the walnut halves. Arrange the walnuts in a dish, the flat sides facing up, place a piece of basil on each, and cover with the parmesan pieces.

STIR-FRIED ASPARAGUS WITH CASHEWS

Although currently popular with Chinese chefs, asparagus has only recently joined the Chinese repertoire. Prepared in this simple way the stalks may accompany many Oriental dishes, such as steamed fish, chicken in black bean sauce, and spicy noodles, serving four. Oyster sauce is available in Oriental stores, or substitute soy sauce.

450g/1lb thin asparagus, washed
4 tbs groundnut oil
4 cloves of garlic, peeled and finely chopped
225g/8oz crisp button mushrooms, sliced
2 tbs Shaohsing wine
2 tbs oyster sauce, or soy sauce
50g/2oz roasted cashews

Snap off the pale, woody base of the asparagus. Roll-cut the asparagus into sections about 2cm/1 inch long, reserving the tips.

Heat the oil in a wok until it smokes. Add the garlic, stir, and add the asparagus and mushrooms. Stir-fry for 2 minutes, then add the Shaohsing wine, oyster sauce, the asparagus tips and cashews. Mix well and stir-fry for 2 more minutes. Serve.

STIR-FRIED GREEN BEANS WITH PEANUTS

With their crunchy texture and gingery flavour, these nutritious beans can accompany most meat, poultry or fish dishes, and serve four.

450g/1lb green beans, washed and trimmed
3 tbs peanut oil
2 cloves of garlic, peeled and finely chopped
2cm/1 inch piece of ginger, peeled and finely chopped
4 spring onions (scallions), washed and sliced
110ml/4 fl oz/½ cup dry white wine
50g/2 oz raw, unsalted peanuts
pinch of sugar
2 tbs soy sauce

Cut the beans into 2cm/1 inch sections.

Heat the oil in a wok until it starts to smoke. Throw in the garlic and ginger. Before they brown, add the beans and spring onions and stir-fry for 2 minutes. Add the wine, peanuts and sugar and continue to stir-fry until the wine has evaporated. Just before serving, add the soy sauce, stir well, and serve.

AUBERGINES (EGGPLANTS) STUFFED
WITH PINE NUTS
· · · · · · · · · ·

A ubergines are very popular in Greece, Turkey, and
the Middle East. Here they are baked with a typ-
ically Middle Eastern stuffing of delicately spiced
minced meat and pine nuts. This is a light main course
for four, accompanied by a colourful salad of radishes,
tomatoes, cucumber, lettuce, red salad onions, olives
and green peppers, dressed with olive oil and lemon
juice. Alternatively, serve the aubergines alone, as an
appetizer.

2 large aubergines, sliced in half from top to bottom
olive oil for frying
1 medium onion, peeled and chopped
small stick (rib) of celery, diced
2 cloves of garlic, peeled and chopped
225g/8oz lean minced lamb or beef
$1/2$ tsp ground cumin
$1/2$ tsp ground cinnamon
salt
freshly milled black pepper
3 canned plum tomatoes, chopped
225ml/8 fl oz/1 cup water
50g/2oz pine nuts
handful of fresh parsley, washed and chopped
2 tbs tomato purée (paste)
140ml/5 fl oz/$2/3$ cup chicken or vegetable stock (broth)

Score the cut sides of the aubergines with 3 or 4
diagonal cuts. Score an equal number of opposing
diagonal cuts, leaving a latticework of cuts. Scoop out
and discard a little of the aubergines' pulpy centres,
taking care to leave a layer of flesh at least 2cm/$3/4$ inch
thick attached to the skins. Briefly fry the aubergines
on both sides in olive oil; remove, and leave them to
cool on paper towel.

Heat about 3 tbs of the oil in a frying pan (discard
or reserve the rest). Sauté the onion, celery and garlic
until soft and lightly coloured. Add the meat and stir-

fry until it has lost all traces of rawness. Add the spices, season, and continue to fry the mixture for 2–3 minutes. Add the tomatoes and the water and simmer for about 35–40 minutes, or until tender, stirring often. Stir in the pine nuts and parsley.

Pre-heat the oven to 190°C/375°F/gas mark 5.

Transfer the aubergines to a large, shallow oven dish, the cut sides facing up. Cover them with the spiced meat and nut mixture. Dissolve the tomato purée in the hot stock. Pour it over the aubergines. Basting from time to time, bake the aubergines for about 20 minutes, and serve hot or warm.

A close relative of skordalia, aïoli and romesco, this pounded garlic and walnut sauce from Turkey can also be made with almonds, hazelnuts, or pine nuts. Like its cousins, tarator is usually served with fried or baked fish, or boiled or fried vegetables. It can be pounded with a mortar and pestle, or made in a food processor, making enough for four.

4–6 cloves of garlic, peeled
2 slices white bread
water
110g/4oz walnuts (shelled weight)
1 tsp salt
juice of $1/_2$ lemon, or 1 tbs wine vinegar
110ml/4 fl oz/$1/_2$ cup fruity olive oil

Simmer the garlic in a little hot oil or boiling water for a few minutes. Reserve it. Soak the bread in a little water, then squeeze out the excess moisture. Pound or process the bread with the garlic, nuts, salt, lemon juice or vinegar, and a little olive oil. Continue to pound or process to a smooth paste, adding the remaining oil in a thin stream.

ROCKET (ARUGULA, RUCOLA) AND ALMOND PESTO

Wild or cultivated rocket can be used in this unusual and quite pungent pesto. Related to mustard, both kinds of rocket have an edible-like peppery taste, although wild rocket is much stronger. Serves four with factory-made penne, or with spaghetti, spaghettini, bucatini or trenette.

1 cup rocket, washed
60g/3oz blanched almonds
handful of fresh parsley, washed
1 small dried chilli
1 clove garlic, peeled
salt
freshly milled black pepper
110ml/4 fl oz/¹/₂ cup extra virgin olive oil

Put all the ingredients except the olive oil in a food processor; process, adding the oil in a stream.

RED PESTO

· · · · · · · · · · ·

This red pesto of sun-dried tomatoes and pine nuts is thick and highly concentrated; it can also be served as a relish for barbecued meat or fowl.

2 tbs lightly toasted pine nuts
8 sun-dried tomato halves
4 tbs extra virgin olive oil
generous handful of fresh parsley
1 clove of garlic, peeled and quartered
½ tsp salt

Combine all the ingredients in a food processor and process thoroughly to a smooth paste. Serves four with pasta and some freshly grated parmesan cheese, or as a relish.

HAZELNUT PESTO CROSTINI

_{· · · · · · · · · ·}

These fragrant crostini are made with pounded hazel-nuts and aromatic flat-leaved parsley; hazelnut pesto is equally delicious with pasta. Serves four.

small loaf of French or Italian bread
50g/2oz hazelnuts (shelled weight)
1 clove of garlic, peeled
$^1/_2$ tsp salt
leaves from a small bunch of fresh parsley
110ml/4 fl oz/$^1/_2$ cup extra virgin olive oil

Pre-heat the oven to 190°C/375°F/gas mark 5. Slice the loaf into slices about 2cm/1 inch thick, and bake them for just a few minutes.

Meanwhile, pound the hazelnuts in a mortar with the garlic, salt and parsley, gradually adding a few drops of the oil. Pound to a paste, then stir in two thirds of the remaining olive oil, reserving some to drizzle over the crostini. (The pesto can also be prepared in a food processor, although the consistency should not be too smooth.) Spread a thick layer of pesto on one side of each lightly baked slice of bread, drizzle with the remaining oil, and return to the oven for a few minutes longer. Serve hot or warm.

Classic Pesto Genovese
. . . .

Pesto made with fragrant basil, olive oil, pine nuts and cheese has become one of the three most popular pasta sauces, alongside Bolognese meat ragù and Neapolitan tomato sauce. It is enjoyed in many different countries, thanks to the availability of commercially made pesto sold in jars; although this is fine as a store-cupboard standby, home-made pesto is hugely superior. Less well known is the Ligurian habit of serving pesto with pasta and waxy salad potatoes. Although one would imagine this to be a heavy combination, in fact the results are very satisfying. It is correct to use a mixture of parmesan and pecorino romano cheeses, but one or other will suffice. Serves four.

a few drops of olive oil
4 small boiling potatoes, cleaned but unpeeled
350g/12oz factory-made linguine, or trenette
loosely packed cup of fresh basil
2 cloves of garlic, peeled and sliced
salt
110g/4oz pine nuts
225ml/8 fl oz/1 cup fruity olive oil
50g/2oz freshly grated parmesan cheese
25g/1oz freshly grated pecorino romano cheese

Bring a very large pot of salted water to the boil, adding a few drops of olive oil. Immerse the potatoes, and after they have cooked for 5 minutes, the linguine. Mix well, and boil until the pasta is *al dente*. The potatoes and the pasta should both be tender, but take care not to overcook them.

Meanwhile, make the pesto; pound or process the basil with the garlic, salt, and pine nuts. Add a little olive oil as soon as you have a pulp. Keep pounding or processing while adding the remaining oil in a thin stream. (If using a mortar and pestle you will have to stir in the oil, so it is best to pound the pesto quite thoroughly with only a little oil before adding the rest.)

When the pasta is almost ready, stir half of the cheese into the pesto. Slice the potatoes. Arrange them around the rim of a hot serving bowl (preferably a shallow one). Drain the pasta (not too thoroughly), and return it to the hot pot. Mix in the pesto, ensuring that all the pasta strands are coated. Transfer to the centre of the serving bowl, sprinkle with the remaining cheese, and serve immediately.

SAFFRON PILAFF WITH TOASTED PINE NUTS

· · · · · · · · · ·

A Turkish pilaff redolent of saffron and flavoured with chicken stock (broth). Serves four with spicy grilled (broiled) meat or poultry, and a salad. Any rice left over is a delicious salad base to which can be added some thinly sliced mushrooms, spring onions (scallions), diced red peppers, and a dressing of olive oil, beaten with wine vinegar and salt.

60g/3oz pine nuts
350g/12oz long-grain rice
450ml/16 fl oz/2 cups home-made chicken stock
generous pinch of saffron strands
salt
handful of fresh parsley, washed and chopped

Lightly toast the pine nuts in a heavy frying pan, tossing and shaking them over a high heat, or toast them under the grill (broiler). Remove and set them aside.

Soak the rice in plenty of fresh water, squeezing gently with your hand to release the starch. Rinse in several changes of cold water, and drain the rice well.

Simmer the stock in another pot. Remove and pour a ladleful of stock into a cup with the saffron. Infuse for 10 minutes. Add a pinch of salt to the stock, the saffron liquid, and the rice. Bring to a simmer, cover tightly, and cook very gently for 15 minutes. Sprinkle with the pine nuts and parsley, fluff with a fork, and serve.

AROMATIC SAFFRON RICE

Serve this perfumed golden rice with lightly spiced, grilled (broiled) chicken, or other Indian dishes. The aroma and flavours of the seeds and spices impregnate the rice as it steams, but the cardamom pods and cinnamon bark should not be eaten. Basmati and Thai fragrant are the most perfumed of long-grained rice varieties and are the best kinds to use. Serves four accompanied by one or more other dishes.

275g/10oz long grain rice
pinch of saffron filaments
350ml/12 fl oz/1½ cups light vegetable or chicken stock
(broth)
1 tsp cumin seeds
1 tsp fennel seeds
1 tsp green cardamom pods
small piece of cinnamon
½ tsp turmeric
1 tsp salt
2 tbs vegetable oil

Wash the rice in frequent changes of fresh water, squeezing the grains gently to release their starch. Drain.

Soak the saffron in a little hot stock for 20 minutes. Toast the cumin seeds lightly in a hot, dry pan. Combine all the ingredients except the saffron and its soaking liquid in a pot. Bring to the boil, and allow the surface of the rice to become pockmarked as the liquid begins to evaporate (this will just take a few minutes). Pour in the saffron and its liquid, mix gently, cover the pot, reduce the heat to very low, and steam for 13–15 minutes. Allow to rest off the heat for a few minutes before serving.

Pumpkin and Hazelnut Risotto
· · · · · · · · · ·

Pumpkins and hazelnuts share the same season, and are plentiful at Halloween. This delicious recipe combines the two very successfully, and puts to good use any spare pumpkin flesh scooped from children's Jack-o'-Lanterns. Serves four.

flesh of 1 medium pumpkin (about 175g/6oz)
110g/4oz hazelnuts, shelled
generous handful of fresh, flat-leaved parsley
2 cloves of garlic, peeled
4 tbs extra virgin olive oil
salt
3 tbs olive oil
1 medium onion, peeled and chopped
275g/10oz peeled canned plum tomatoes, chopped
salt
freshly milled black pepper
275g/10oz/1½ cups arborio rice
1 litre/2¼ pints/4½ cups chicken stock (broth)
110g/4oz freshly grated parmesan cheese

Remove and discard its seeds and fibres, and coarsely chop the pumpkin flesh.

Pound the hazelnuts, parsley and garlic with a mortar and pestle (or process them to a paste). Add the olive oil a tablespoon at a time, mixing well. Season with a pinch of salt, mix well, and reserve.

Heat the remaining olive oil in a large, heavy pan and fry the onion until it colours a little. Add the pumpkin and continue to sauté for about 4 minutes. Mix in the hazelnut paste. Add the tomatoes, mix well, and simmer until they thicken. Season and mix. Add the rice, and stir-fry for a minute or two. Add the hot stock in stages, stirring well each time. Allowing the rice almost to dry out before each fresh addition, use up all the stock in this way; the risotto is ready when it is no longer soupy, and the rice is tender while retaining a very slight firmness in the centre of each grain. (This should take about 25 minutes.) Transfer to a warmed serving dish, mix in half of the parmesan, and serve with the rest of the cheese.

BLUE CHEESE, CELERY AND HAZELNUT SOUP
·········

This delicious soup thickened with crushed nuts can be made with many kinds of soft, mature blue-veined cheese, such as English Stilton, or Italian dolcelatte, and crushed walnuts can be substituted. Serves four.

2 tbs olive oil
12g/½oz butter
2 sticks (ribs) of celery, finely diced
2 cloves of garlic, peeled and finely chopped
110g/4oz Stilton, or dolcelatte cheese, cubed
12 hazelnuts, shelled, and crushed with a mortar and pestle
salt
freshly milled black pepper
225 ml/8 fl oz/1 cup milk
450ml/1 pint/2 cups hot chicken or vegetable stock (broth)
2 tbs dry sherry
40g/1½oz freshly grated parmesan cheese

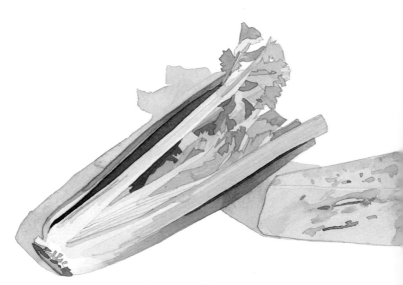

Heat the olive oil and the butter in a pot. Before the fat smokes, add the celery; soften it over a medium heat for a few minutes. Add the garlic, mix well, and simmer for a minute longer. Add the cheese. When this has almost melted, add the crushed nuts, season, and mix well. Pour in the milk, the stock and the sherry. Mix well, bring just to the boil, reduce to a simmer, and cook gently for 15 minutes. Stir in the parmesan, mix well, and serve hot, with croûtons.

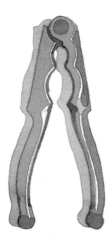

Variation: pasta sauce

If the quantity of milk is reduced by half, and the stock and sherry are omitted, this recipe also makes a wonderful sauce for fresh or dried pasta. Simmer the ingredients for only 8 minutes after the milk has been added. Boil the pasta separately until *al ∂ente*, drain it well, and combine it with the bubbling sauce, to coat; serve with additional freshly grated parmesan cheese.

WINTER SALAD WITH WALNUTS AND GOAT'S CHEESE
··········

This elegant salad of winter vegetables combines pleasant, contrasting textures of crunchy nuts, crisp leaves and melting fried goat's cheese. The red, white, green and orange vegetables provide plenty of colour. Serves four as an appetizer.

10 walnuts
8 leaves of chicory (Belgian endive)
10 leaves of red radicchio
heart of a lettuce
1 large carrot, scrubbed
2 sticks (ribs) of celery
2 medium goat's cheeses (200g/7oz total weight)
flour
olive oil for frying
5 tbs extra virgin olive oil (or walnut oil)
2 tbs white wine or champagne vinegar
pinch of sugar
$^1\!/_2$ tsp salt

Stand the walnuts upright on a sturdy surface. Smash the pointed ends open with a hammer and prize out the kernels (meats); roughly chop them.

Wash all the vegetables and shake them dry. If necessary, blot away the remaining moisture with paper towel. Tear the leaves roughly. Grate the carrot coarsely. Slice the celery thinly. Combine all the vegetables in a bowl.

Cut the goat's cheese into sections each about 5 x 3cm/2 x 1¼ inches. Roll them in flour. Heat a generous layer of olive oil in a non-stick frying pan. When just smoking, add the cheese sections. Fry them until evenly golden, and the centres start to ooze (this will just take a couple of minutes). Remove and reserve.

Beat the extra virgin olive oil or walnut oil with the vinegar, sugar and salt. Pour over the vegetables and mix well. Divide the dressed vegetables and arrange them attractively on four small plates. Scatter the walnut pieces over them and arrange pieces of fried cheese in the centre of each portion. Serve immediately.

Walnut Bread

Although it is a very good substitute for ordinary bread, walnut bread is especially delicious with cheese. These quantities make two ½kg/1lb loaves which freeze very well.

450g/1lb/4 cups wholemeal flour
225g/8oz/2 cups plain (all purpose) flour
1 tbs salt
7g/¼ oz sachet fast-action dried yeast
1 tbs sunflower oil
1 tbs black treacle (molasses)
450 ml/16 fl oz/2 cups warm water
110g/4 oz walnut kernels (meats), coarsely chopped

Sift the flour and salt into a large, warm bowl. Add the dried yeast, oil, treacle and water to the flour, and, if using a dough hook, machine-knead the mixture at slow speed for about 4 minutes, or until the dough is quite smooth and leaves the side of the bowl cleanly. (If kneading the dough by hand, this will take 10-15 minutes.) Add the chopped walnuts to the dough and mix thoroughly. Cover the bowl with a damp cloth and let the dough rise in a warm place until it has roughly doubled in size. Divide it in half and shape each piece of dough in an oiled loaf tin (pan).

Meanwhile, pre-heat the oven to 190°C/375°F/gas mark 5. Bake for 15 minutes, then reduce the heat to 180°C/350°F/gas mark 4 and continue to bake for a further 20 minutes; by then the loaves will have browned and should sound hollow when tapped.

WALNUT SAUCE FOR PASTA
· · · · · · · · · ·

Make this with the new season's 'wet' walnuts, if available. (Dry, stored walnuts can be substituted.) Select pasta shapes to which the sauce will cling, such as fusilli, garganelli or penne rigate. This serves four people as a first course, or two as a complete light meal, accompanied by a salad and crusty bread.

14 walnuts
350g/12oz factory-made (or more fresh egg) pasta
2 tbs walnut or olive oil
3 cloves of garlic, peeled and finely chopped
salt
freshly milled black pepper
3 tbs milk
3 tbs concentrated crème fraîche, or 4 tbs fromage frais
50g/2oz parmesan cheese, freshly grated
12 fresh basil leaves, roughly torn

Stand the walnuts upright on a solid surface, and tap the pointed ends smartly with a hammer, to smash the shells. Prize out the kernels (meats), and roughly chop them.

Bring a very large pot of salted water to the boil. Immerse the pasta and cook until *al dente* while you make the sauce. (If using fresh pasta, delay this step until the sauce is nearly ready, and boil it for just 3 minutes, or until tender. Fresh egg pasta that has been dried for storage will need about 10 minutes' boiling.)

Heat the oil in a frying pan with the walnuts and garlic. Sauté them gently for 2–3 minutes. Season well. Pour in the milk and the crème fraîche or fromage frais, and half of the parmesan cheese. Allow the sauce to thicken for about 3 minutes, then add the basil. Drain the pasta and combine it with the sauce. Serve with the remaining parmesan.

Coconut Curried Noodles with Vegetables

....

A steaming platter of delicious noodles and morsels of tender vegetables curried in coconut milk. Use any dried or fresh Oriental noodles, but be sure to follow the cooking instructions; they should be just tender before going into the wok, and while most thin rice noodles only need a brief immersion in boiling water, others, such as dried egg noodles may require more prolonged boiling. Fresh egg noodles can be used straight from the packet. Bottled Thai or Vietnamese fish sauce can be obtained in Oriental stores. This is a complete light lunch or supper for four, or serve it as an appetizer for six.

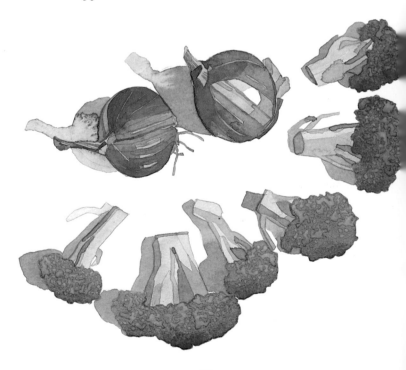

900g/2lb fresh, or 350g/12oz dried, Oriental noodles
6–8 broccoli florets
10 green beans, trimmed
4 tbs peanut oil
1 medium aubergine (eggplant), diced
110g/4oz button mushrooms, sliced
2 fresh chillies, washed, seeded and sliced
6–8 small red shallots (or 3–4 yellow shallots), peeled and
chopped
3 cloves of garlic, peeled and finely chopped
2 tsp curry paste
280ml/10 fl oz/1 1/4 cups canned coconut milk
1 tsp sugar
1 tbs fish sauce
1 tbs light soy sauce
heart of a crisp lettuce, shredded
handful of fresh coriander (cilantro), washed and chopped
50g/2oz roasted cashews, roughly chopped

Reconstitute and soften the dried noodles, following the packet instructions. Lightly par-boil the broccoli and the green beans, then refresh them in cold water. Drain them well. Divide the florets into small pieces. Cut the beans into 2cm/1 inch lengths.

Heat the oil to smoking point in a wok. Add the vegetables and stir-fry for a minute. Add the chillies, shallots and garlic, and stir-fry them for a minute before adding the curry paste. Stir this into the vegetables and pour in the coconut milk. Add the sugar, and the fish and soy sauces. Mix well and add the noodles. Toss these in the sauce for about 2 minutes, to heat through, and transfer to a warm serving platter, surrounding the noodles with the shredded lettuce. Sprinkle with the coriander and cashews and serve immediately.

Prawn (Shrimp) Curry with Macadamia Nuts
· · · · · · · · · ·

Raw tiger prawns are perfect in this quick, delicious dish, although other raw prawns can be substituted. Bottled Thai or Vietnamese fish sauce can be found in Oriental stores. Serves four with plain boiled rice to soak up the rich sauce. Grated lemon peel can be used instead of lemon grass.

50g/2oz shelled macadamia nuts
450g/1lb large raw prawns (thawed if previously frozen)
3 cloves garlic, peeled
6 red shallots (or 3 yellow shallots), peeled
small piece of fresh ginger, or galangal, peeled
1 stalk of fresh lemon grass, thinly sliced, *or*
grated peel of half a lemon
3 tbs light vegetable oil
3 tbs water
$1/2$ tsp cayenne
$1/2$ tsp turmeric
280ml/10 fl oz/$1 1/4$ cups
canned coconut milk
1 tbs fish sauce
1 tbs light soy sauce
$1/2$ tsp sugar
2 fresh chillies, seeded and halved vertically
leaves from 2–3 sprigs of fresh basil

Grind the nuts with a mortar and pestle, or in a clean coffee grinder. Shell the prawns. Process the garlic and shallots to a paste with the ginger or galangal, lemon grass or grated lemon peel, oil and water. Transfer the paste to a very hot wok and stir-fry until it darkens a little. Add the cayenne and turmeric, prawns and nuts, and toss them briefly in the paste, to coat. Add the coconut milk, fish and soy sauces, and the sugar; cook until the oil just starts to separate from the sauce which, after 5 minutes or so will have thickened somewhat. Garnish with the chillies and basil and serve immediately.

STEAMED SEA BASS WITH SESAME SEEDS
· · · · · · · · · ·

This opulent dish serves four with plain boiled rice and one or more Oriental dishes, including some stir-fried vegetables in oyster sauce. Look for a sea bass or a striped bass weighing about 800g/1³/₄lb.

1 medium bass, gutted, cleaned and scaled
salt
freshly milled black pepper
2cm/1 inch piece of fresh ginger, peeled and finely chopped
4 spring onions (scallions), washed and thinly sliced
2 cloves of garlic, peeled and finely chopped
1 fresh green or red chilli, seeded and thinly sliced
4 tbs peanut oil
3 tbs sesame seeds, lightly toasted
3 tsp Shaohsing wine, or sherry
2 tsp sesame oil
2 tbs light soy sauce

Wash the fish in running water and pat it dry. Season it inside and out. Slash both sides diagonally two or three times with a sharp knife. If steaming in a wok, place the fish on a plate or platter, and stand that on a trivet. (If the fish is too big for the wok, trim off a large part of the tail with scissors, or cut the fish in two and lay the halves side by side on the plate.) Pour enough water into the wok to come up its sides without reaching the plate (or use a steamer).

Scatter all the vegetables over and around the fish, bring the water to the boil, cover the wok, and reduce to a simmer. Steam until the flesh is flaky and the fish's eyes are white (about 10 minutes). Carefully drain off the excess water that will have condensed on to the plate. Cover the wok again, without turning on the heat.

Heat the peanut oil in a small pan until it begins to smoke. Put in the sesame seeds and immediately pour the oil and the seeds over the fish to complete the cooking, adding the Shaohsing wine, sesame oil, and soy sauce. Serve from the hot platter.

CHICKEN STEW WITH PEANUTS

A spicy stew from West Africa, where peanuts are an important crop and are frequently used to thicken sauces, or stewed alone. Serves four.

4 tbs groundnut oil
1 corn-fed chicken, in serving pieces
1 onion, peeled and finely chopped
2 cloves of garlic, peeled and finely chopped
small piece of fresh ginger, peeled and finely chopped
2–3 fresh chillies, washed, seeded and thinly sliced
6 tbs chopped canned tomatoes
small piece of cinnamon bark
1 tsp ground cumin
110g/4oz roasted peanuts, crushed
salt
freshly milled black pepper
225ml/8 fl oz/1 cup water

Heat the oil in a heavy stewing pot. Brown the chicken pieces all over, remove and reserve them.

Fry the onion until golden; add the garlic, ginger and chillies, and mix well. Add the tomatoes and remaining spices, and fry for a minute or two. Add the peanuts, mix, season, and return the chicken to the pot. Pour in the water, bring to the boil, and cover. Reduce to a simmer and cook for 25 minutes. Serve with rice, potatoes or bread.

CHICKEN SATAY WITH PEANUT SAUCE
· · · · · · · · · ·

This is a marvellous appetizer for six, or a complete meal for four, served with plenty of plain boiled rice. Spicy grilled (broiled) chicken, flavoured with tangy south east Asian spices and condiments is invariably served with peanut sauce and a sweet, hot, sour and nutty carrot and cucumber salad. (Bottled Thai or Vietnamese fish sauce is obtainable in Oriental stores.) In this version the chicken is marinated in a mixture that includes cream, which, although alien to southeast Asia, tenderizes the chicken to a delightfully melting consistency. Satay may also be made with pork or beef. It is best barbecued over charcoal or wood embers, but may also be grilled.

Garam masala
4 cloves
1 tsp cumin seeds
2cm/1 inch of cinnamon
1 tsp fennel seeds
seeds from 1 tsp cardamom pods
2 tsp coriander seeds
1 tsp black peppercorns

Pound the spices in a mortar and pestle, or grind them in a clean coffee grinder.

Marinade
4 chicken breasts
4 cloves of garlic, peeled and crushed
2cm/1 inch piece of ginger, peeled and finely chopped
2 tbs peanut oil
4 tbs single (light) cream
1 tbs garam masala
1 tsp cayenne
1 tsp turmeric
1 tbs soy sauce
1 tbs fish sauce
salt
freshly milled black pepper
juice of ½ a lemon

Skin the chicken breasts and slice them into strips about 1cm/¹/₂ inch wide. Put them into a bowl and add the remaining marinade ingredients. Mix thoroughly, cover, and leave for at least an hour.

Meanwhile, make the peanut sauce.

Peanut sauce
4 tbs peanut oil
1 small onion, peeled and finely chopped
2 cloves of garlic, peeled and finely chopped
4 tbs peanut butter
4 tbs coconut milk
225ml/8 fl oz/1 cup water
1 tbs sugar
1 tsp cayenne
1 tsp turmeric
1 tbs fish sauce
1 tbs soy sauce

Heat the oil and fry the onion and garlic. Before they brown, add the peanut butter and fry for a minute or so longer, then add the remaining ingredients, mix well, and simmer for 30 minutes, or until the oil separates from the sauce.

Thread the chicken slices on to skewers, then grill, barbecue, or cook on a hot griddle, turning a few times to ensure all sides are golden. Baste with the remaining marinade. Serve the peanut sauce and carrot and cucumber salad in separate bowls.

CARROT AND CUCUMBER SALAD
· · · · · · · · · ·

This nutty relish traditionally accompanies satay.

$^{1}/_{2}$ cucumber, peeled, washed and halved
2 medium carrots, scrubbed, halved and thinly sliced
2 tbs sugar
2 tbs rice vinegar
2 dried red chillies, crumbled
2 spring onions (scallions) washed and sliced
handful of coriander (cilantro), washed and sliced
50g/2oz roasted peanuts, crushed

Remove the seedy centre from the cucumber with a teaspoon, and discard it. Slice the flesh thinly

Put the carrots and cucumber into a bowl. Combine the sugar with the vinegar, stirring thoroughly until the sugar granules have dissolved. Pour the liquid over the vegetables. Sprinkle with the chillies, spring onion, coriander and peanuts.

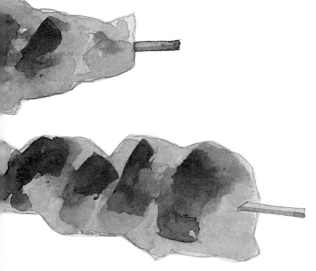

TURKEY MOLE

· · · · · · · · · · ·

This festive Mexican dish combines five important foods introduced into the Old World by the Spaniards: peanuts, turkey, chillies, tomatoes and chocolate. Although mole (which means 'sauce') is made with turkey at Christmas and on other festive occasions, chicken is an excellent substitute on less grand occasions, but requires a shorter cooking time. The main recipe for a medium turkey serves ten people, and is an impressive dish for entertaining. The second recipe is for a medium chicken and serves four. Accompany either version with rice, refried beans and corn tortilla chips.

boned meat of a medium turkey (about 1kg/2¼lb)
50g/2oz sesame seeds
50g/2oz whole blanched almonds
50g/2oz raw, unsalted peanuts
enough dried, mild chillies to fill a small bowl
(ancho, mulato, pasilla and chipotle, if available) *or*
1–2 tbs small, dried, extra hot chillies
8cm/3 inch piece of cinnamon
2 tsp cumin seeds
110 ml/4 fl oz/½ cup sunflower oil
3 medium onions, peeled and chopped
6 cloves of garlic, peeled and finely chopped
5 tbs red wine vinegar
1 tsp sugar
1 litre/2¼ pints/4½ cups chicken stock (broth)
400g/14oz canned plum tomatoes, chopped
salt
freshly milled black pepper
pinch of oregano
25g/1oz grated chocolate

Cut the turkey meat into large, even chunks. Toast the sesame seeds and the nuts in a heavy pan until lightly coloured. Remove and reserve them. Grind the chillies and spices with a mortar and pestle, or in a clean coffee grinder.

Heat the oil in a very large, lidded casserole. Fry the turkey pieces until they are evenly golden. Remove and reserve them. Add the onions and fry until lightly coloured. Add the garlic and the ground chillies and spices, mix well, and sauté gently for a few minutes longer. Return the turkey to the casserole and mix well, to coat. Add the vinegar, sugar, chicken stock and tomatoes, and season with salt, pepper and oregano. Simmer for about 40 minutes, stirring a few times. Add the grated chocolate and the toasted nuts, mix well, and continue to simmer, uncovered, for up to half an hour longer, or until the turkey is tender and the sauce has thickened and darkened. Serve.

Chicken mole

Divide a chicken weighing approximately 1½kg/ 3¼lb into two whole breast and leg portions, then proceed as in the main recipe, but reduce the quantities of all the other ingredients by half. Simmer the chicken pieces (uncovered) in the sauce for only 25 minutes, then for up to 15 more minutes after the nuts and the chocolate have been added.

CHICKEN CASSEROLE WITH
HAZELNUT PICADA
· · · · · · · · · ·

Catalans thicken their stews and casseroles with picadas, aromatic nut pastes flavoured with fresh herbs and garlic. Serves four.

1 large, corn-fed chicken
4 tbs olive oil
1 medium onion, peeled and chopped
1 carrot, peeled and diced
1 stick (rib) of celery, diced
225g/8 oz large button mushrooms, quartered
1½ tbs tomato purée (paste)
6 tbs white wine
3–4 tbs dry sherry
salt
freshly milled black pepper

Picada
2 cloves of garlic, peeled
50g/2oz hazelnuts (shelled weight)
handful of fresh parsley, washed
2 tbs extra virgin olive oil
pinch of salt

Cut the chicken into large serving pieces. Heat the olive oil in a heavy, lidded casserole. Brown the chicken pieces evenly, and transfer them to a plate.

Sauté the onion, carrot and celery in the oil for a few minutes. Add the mushrooms and sauté them for 4–5 minutes. Return the chicken pieces, add the tomato purée, pour in the wine and sherry, season, and bring to the boil. Reduce the heat, cover, and simmer for 20 minutes.

Meanwhile, pound the picada ingredients with a mortar and pestle, stirring in the oil when the nuts are reduced to a coarse paste (or grind all the ingredients in a food processor). Add the picada to the casserole, mix well, and continue to simmer with the lid ajar for 15 more minutes. Serve with potatoes.

CHICKEN BREASTS SAUTÉED WITH PINE NUTS

· · · · · · · · · ·

This aromatic and tasty dish takes just a few minutes to cook. The chicken breasts are first sliced so as to cook quickly as the sauce thickens. Serves four with potatoes and a vegetable.

4 corn-fed chicken breasts, with skins on
4 tbs olive oil
sprig each of thyme and rosemary
peel and juice of 1 lime (or $\frac{1}{2}$ a lemon)
60g/3oz pine nuts, lightly toasted
1 tbs capers, rinsed and drained
2 cloves of garlic, peeled and finely chopped
110ml/4 fl oz/$\frac{1}{2}$ cup white wine
salt
freshly milled black pepper

Cut each breast into thick strips.

Heat the olive oil in a well-seasoned frying pan; fry the chicken pieces with the herbs until they are golden all over. Add the remaining ingredients and bring to a boil. Reduce the heat to medium and let the sauce thicken while the chicken pieces finish cooking (this will only take 5–6 minutes). Discard the herbs; serve the chicken, with its scarce sauce, on warmed plates.

Chestnut Pavé

. . . .

If top quality chocolate with a high content of cocoa solids is used, this pavé will taste sensational. A combination of caster (superfine) sugar and a teaspoon of vanilla essence can replace the vanilla sugar; this is sugar that has been stored in a sealed jar with real vanilla pods (beans). Peeled, vacuum-packed chestnuts are sometimes available, but peeling chestnuts is relatively easy if they are fried and roasted first. Serves at least six as the pavé is dense and rich.

575g/1¼ lb chestnuts (225g/8oz peeled weight)
1 tbs groundnut oil
110g/4oz dark chocolate
6 tbs water
75g/3oz vanilla sugar
75g/3oz butter, at room temperature
1 tbs brandy
1 tbs grated orange peel

Preheat the oven to 180°C/350°F/gas mark 4. With a sharp knife score a cross on the flat side of each chestnut. Heat the oil in a large pan with an ovenproof handle, add the chestnuts, and stir them until they sizzle. Transfer the pan to the oven and bake for about 20 minutes. This will loosen the shells and skins to allow the soft chestnuts to be peeled relatively easily.

Finely grind the chestnuts in a food processor. Melt the chocolate in a small pan with the water and allow the mixture to cool. Beat together the sugar and butter. Combine all the ingredients and pack the mixture into a 20cm/8 inch oblong baking tin (pan) with steep sides, lined with oiled greaseproof (waxed) paper. Refrigerate for at least 24 hours.

To serve, invert the pavé on to a serving dish, top with whipped double cream, dust with cocoa powder, and cut into serving slices.

PECAN PIE

· · · · · · · · · ·

An American classic, pecan pie is very easy to make. There is no better accompaniment than a generous helping of top quality vanilla ice cream. A good pecan pie should be dense, moist and rich. Vanilla essence can be replaced by caster (superfine) sugar that has been stored in a sealed jar with some vanilla pods (beans) Makes a pie big enough for six generous helpings.

flour
225g/8oz short crust pastry (tart dough)
1 cup baking beans
2 eggs
175g/6oz caster sugar
pinch of salt
1 tsp vanilla essence (see above)
25g/1oz butter, melted
4 tbs golden syrup (dark corn syrup)
110g/4oz shelled pecans, chopped
25g/1oz shelled pecans, halved

Pre-heat the oven to 220°C/425°F/gas mark 7. Apply a little flour to a clean work surface and roll out the pastry to fit a 23cm/9 inch flan tin (tart pan). Line the tin with the pastry and trim off any jagged edges. Prick the pastry base with a fork. Line the pastry with a sheet of greaseproof (waxed) paper, and weigh down with the baking beans. Bake blind for 10 minutes. Remove the paper and the baking beans.

Meanwhile, lightly beat the eggs in a large bowl. Mix in the sugar, salt, vanilla essence (if using), butter, syrup and chopped pecans. Mix thoroughly. Pour the mixture into the pastry case, and cover with the pecan halves. Bake for 15 minutes, then reduce the temperature to 180°C/350°F/gas mark 4 and continue to bake for 15–20 more minutes, or until set. Allow to cool slightly, and serve warm, or cold.

BAKLAVAS

T his best known of Greek pastries is probably very ancient. During the Ottoman Empire, it was introduced into other Middle Eastern countries where it is ubiquitous today. Stuffed with nuts and drenched in honey, even sweet desserts like this one can be good for you. Walnuts or almonds can replace the pistachio nuts. Filo pastry is extremely difficult to make but just about everybody uses the frozen kind. Serves four.

225g/8oz shelled pistachios
1 tsp ground cinnamon
melted butter, or light oil, to grease the pastry sheets
350g/12oz frozen filo pastry, (14–16 sheets), thawed
a little milk
175g/6oz sugar
170ml/6 fl oz/³/₄ cup water
small piece of cinnamon
1 tbs lemon juice
6 tbs clear honey

Preheat the oven to 190°C/375°F/gas mark 5. Spread the pistachios out on a firm surface and cover them with a clean cloth, or paper towel. Beat them with a hammer to lightly crush them. Combine them in a small bowl with the ground cinnamon.

Lightly grease a shallow baking tin (pan) measuring approximately 20cm/8 inches square, and cover with 6 lightly greased sheets of filo pastry (let the edges overhang the sides of the tin as they will be folded over the pastry). Spoon in half of the nut filling. Cover with 4 more lightly greased sheets, followed by the remaining nuts. Fold over the overhanging pastry layers, and cover with the remaining greased sheets. Score a cross through the pastry without cutting through to the base, dividing it into quarters.

Brush the pastry with milk. Transfer to the oven and bake for 25–35 minutes, or until the surface is a deep golden brown. Remove and let it cool.

Make a syrup by combining the sugar, water, the piece of cinnamon, lemon juice, and 2 tbs of the honey. Bring to the boil, reduce the heat, and simmer for about 8 minutes, or until it has thickened. Mix in the remaining honey and simmer for another 2-3 minutes. Pour the syrup over the baklavas and allow it to cool. Serve when most of the syrup has been absorbed by the baklavas. (Refrigerated, this will keep for a couple of days.)

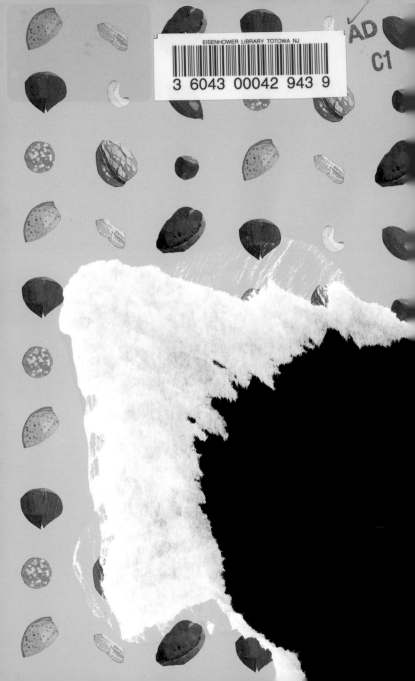